Pebble®

Families

Uncles

Revised and Updated

by Lola M. Schaefer

Consulting Editor: Gail Saunders-Smith, PhD

Capstone
press®

Mankato, Minnesota

Pebble Books are published by Capstone Press,
151 Good Counsel Drive, P.O. Box 669, Mankato, Minnesota 56002.
www.capstonepub.com

Books published by Capstone Press are manufactured with paper
containing at least 10 percent post-consumer waste.

Library of Congress Cataloging-in-Publication Data
Schaefer, Lola M., 1950–
    Uncles / by Lola M. Schaefer. — Rev. and updated.
    p. cm. — (Pebble books. Families)
    Includes bibliographical references and index.
    Summary: "Simple text and photographs present uncles and how they interact
with their families" — Provided by publisher.
    ISBN-13: 978-1-4296-1229-6 (hardcover)   ISBN-10: 1-4296-1229-0 (hardcover)
    ISBN-13: 978-1-4296-1758-1 (softcover)   ISBN-10: 1-4296-1758-6 (softcover)
    1. Uncles — Juvenile literature. I. Title. II. Series.
HQ759.94.S35 2008
306.87 — dc22   2007027103

Note to Parents and Teachers

The Families set supports national social studies standards related
to identifying family members and their roles in the family. This
book describes and illustrates uncles. The images support early
readers in understanding the text. The repetition of words and
phrases helps early readers learn new words. This book also
introduces early readers to subject-specific vocabulary words, which
are defined in the glossary section. Early readers may need some
assistance to read some words and to use the Table of Contents,
Glossary, Read More, Internet Sites, and Index sections of the book.

Printed in the United States of America in Stevens Point, Wisconsin.
062011   006237

Table of Contents

Uncles

Uncles are brothers
of mothers and fathers.

brothers

uncle

father

daughter

niece

Uncles live nearby
or far away.

Nieces and Nephews

Uncles have nieces
and nephews.

What Uncles Do

Uncle Kyle plays the guitar.

Uncle Tony plays basketball.

Uncle Ted puts together
a puzzle.

Uncle Marc cooks
for a picnic.

18

Uncle Jeff laughs.

Uncles love.

Glossary

brother — a boy or a man who has the same parents as another child

father — a male parent; an uncle is your father's brother.

mother — a female parent; an uncle is your mother's brother.

nephew — the son of an uncle's brother or sister

niece — the daughter of an uncle's brother or sister